**ABUNDANT TRUTH INTERNATIONAL MINISTRIES**

Biblical Studies Series

# If You Have Seen Me, You Have Seen the Father

## Understanding the Fullness of the Godhead

**Roderick Levi Evans**

**If You Have Seen Me, You Have Seen the Father**
*Understanding The Fullness of the Godhead*

All Rights Reserved ©2008 by Roderick L. Evans

Front & Back Cover Designs by Abundant Truth Publishing All Rights Reserved.
Image by Meranda D from Pixabay

Abundant Truth Publishing
an imprint of Abundant Truth International Ministries

For information address:
Abundant Truth International
P.O. Box 126
Camden, NC 27921

Unless otherwise indicated, all of the scripture quotations are taken from the *Authorized King James Version* **of the Bible.** Scripture quotations marked with NIV are taken from the *New International Version* **of the Bible.** Scripture quotations marked with ASV are taken from the *American Standard Version* **of the Bible.** Scripture quotations marked with GW are taken from the *God's Word Bible.*

ISBN-13 : 978-1601416216

Printed in the United States of America.

# Contents

Introduction

**Lesson 1 – Divine Communications    1**

The Progenitor Speaks to the Progeny   12

The Progeny Spoke to the Progenitor   21

**Lesson 2 – The Divine and the    31
Disciples' Witness**

The Witness of the Fallen Angels    35

The Witness of God and Father    40

The Witness of the Only Begotten    48

The Witness of Christ's Messengers    51

**Lesson 3 – Views and Visions    61**

Daniel's Coronation Vision    68

Jesus' View of His Commission    76

# Contents (cont.)

The Apostles' View of the Divine Persons     79

**Bibliography**     **91**

# Introduction

Paul instructed Timothy to rightly divide the Word of Truth. In order to do this as believers we should follow this example and become students of the Bible. The Biblical Studies Series was developed to aid believers in the study of the various scriptures and foundational doctrines.

**In this publication:**

In this study, we will explore foundational truths concerning the Godhead; that is the divine nature. We know that the nature of God eternally exists in three Persons: The Father, the Son, and the Holy Spirit.

However, at the core of the Godhead is the relationship between the Father and the Son. In this study, we will look exclusively at the relationship and correlation between the Father and Son. It is our hope this information will give a foundation to the doctrine of the Trinity.

If You Have Seen Me, You Have Seen the Father

# -Lesson 1-
# Divine Communications
## Psalm 110:1

If You Have Seen Me, You Have Seen the Father

During His earthly ministry, Jesus faced constant criticism and opposition from the religious leaders of the day. The Pharisees and Sadducees tried to undermine Him through deceitful questions; hoping to trap Him in His words.

However, Jesus consistently confounded them. The gospels record that those that heard Him were always "astonished at His doctrine."

*And when the multitude heard this, they were astonished at his doctrine. Matt 22:33 (KJV)*

After one of these instances, Jesus confronted the Pharisees with their own devices. He asked them a question. Matthew records,

> *While the Pharisees were gathered together, Jesus asked them, Saying, What think ye of Christ? Whose son is he? They say unto him, The Son of David. He saith unto them, How then doth David in spirit call him Lord, saying, The LORD said unto my Lord, Sit thou on my right hand, till I make thine enemies thy footstool? If David then call him Lord, how is he his son?*

*And no man was able to answer him a word, neither durst any man from that day forth ask him any more questions. Matt 22:41-46 (KJV)*

Christ's words establish biblical truths concerning the Jewish understanding of the Messiah, David's connection to the Messiah, and the interpersonal dynamics of the relationship between the Father and the Son.

The Jewish people understood that the Christ would be the descendant of David. They understood that He would be a righteous King who would bring restoration and deliverance to God's people. However, they did not fully comprehend the deity of the promised Messiah.

Remember, David was a prophet and king, so they could understand that the Messiah would come as God's messenger in conjunction with His rule. Yet, they missed the spiritual implications of His coming; that is, He would come as the only begotten Son of God.

Though there is much to be explored concerning these truths, we must turn our attention towards the latter parts of Jesus' statements. Amid His challenge, He quotes one of the Psalms,

> *The LORD said unto my Lord, Sit thou at my right hand, until I make thine enemies thy footstool. Psalms 110:1 (KJV)*

This verse not only reveals the deity of Christ, but it also demonstrates to us the interpersonal relationship of the Father and the Son. We see that there are conversations that take place between them. This is a direct contradiction of the belief that God and Jesus Christ are one and the same.

Though they are one, they are distinctive in existence. Though Jesus used this verse to establish His deity, we discover it solidifies the eternal existence of the Father and the Son; characterized by heavenly communication.

Some have tried to reconcile this verse with the Oneness doctrine by implying that it is an instance of God speaking to Himself. However, the words are clear that God is not saying to Himself to sit at His own right hand.

It does not make sense. In addition, we do have an account of God speaking concerning Himself in His promise to Abraham,

> *And said, By myself have I sworn, saith the LORD, for because thou hast done this thing, and hast not withheld thy son, thine only son: That in blessing I will bless thee, and in multiplying I will multiply thy seed as the stars of the heaven, and as the sand which is upon the sea shore; and thy seed shall possess the gate of his enemies. Gen 22:16-17 (KJV)*

So, we discover that if God spoke to Himself or concerning Himself, it can be understood plainly, not needing any search for interpretation. Furthermore, looking at the construction of Psalm 110:1, in the Hebrew language, dissolves any doubt that God was speaking to and of another; that is, Christ. Let's look at the verse again.

> *The LORD said unto my Lord, Sit thou at my right hand, until I make thine enemies thy footstool. Psalms 110:1 (KJV)*

In the English translations, we see the word Lord used twice (Lord said unto my Lord). However, in the Hebrew two different words are used for Lord. The first 'Lord' in this verse is the Hebrew word Yahweh or Jehovah, the same name God used to reveal Himself to Moses as the Self-Existent or Eternal God.

The second 'Lord' in this verse is the Hebrew word Adonai, which means King or Master. Hence, the verse reads in this sense, "The Eternal God said to the King…" Numerous passages of scriptures attest to the kingship and lordship of Christ. He is repeatedly called king, ruler, lord, and master.

*Therefore let all the house of Israel*

*know assuredly, that God hath made that same Jesus, whom ye have crucified, both Lord and Christ. Acts 2:36 (KJV)*

Hence, we understand that God was speaking to the Son whom He made 'king of kings' and 'lord of lords.' In addition to the verse in Psalm 110, other scriptures establish the distinct personalities of the Father, the Son, and the Holy Spirit in interpersonal communication.

**The Progenitor Speaks to the Progeny**

Both Testaments give record of the Father speaking to Jesus Christ. As we examine these, we further establish the uniqueness of the Father and the Son. Many of David's psalms included prophecies concerning the Messiah.

As with Psalm 110, other psalms prophetically reveal communication between the Father and the Son. Even the latter part of Psalm 110 reveals more communication of the Father towards the Son.

*The LORD hath sworn, and will not repent, Thou art a priest for ever after the order of Melchizedek. Psalms 110:4 (KJV)*

After declaring the kingship of Christ whose enemies will be conquered, David continues by prophetically showing the Father establishing Christ's priesthood. The Father gave an oath concerning the priesthood of Christ. He told Christ that He was a priest after the order of Melchizedek. The writer of Hebrews establishes that this verse is expressly speaking of God talking to Christ.

*So also Christ glorified not himself to be made an high priest; but he that said unto him, Thou art my Son, today have I begotten thee. As he saith also*

> *in another place, Thou art a priest for ever after the order of Melchisedec. Heb 5:5-6 (KJV)*

Again, the construction of this verse in Psalm 110 portrays God talking to Christ and not of Christ (demonstrated by God saying, "thou"). When Christ entered the world, therefore He said,

> *For I have not spoken of myself; but the Father which sent me, he gave me a commandment, what I should say, and what I should speak. And I know that his commandment is life everlasting: whatsoever I speak*

*therefore, even as the Father said unto me, so I speak. John 12:49-50 (KJV)*

Christ testified that everything He said and did, He did at the command of the Father. Though the Son is eternal like the Father, He is always seen in subjection to Him.

This explains why we have record of conversations that establish this truth. Hence, Christ refers to Himself as a king and priest because the Father decreed it. He calls Himself the Son of God because the Father called Him, Son.

*God hath fulfilled the same unto us their children, in that he hath raised up Jesus again; as it is also written in the second psalm, Thou art my Son, this day have I begotten thee. Acts 13:33 (KJV)*

We see Paul quoting Psalm 2 which reveals that the Father said to Jesus that He was God's 'Son.' This along with the aforementioned verses all derived from Old Testament passages. Nevertheless, these verses do not stand alone.

In the New Testament, we find that God publicly and not prophetically speaks to and of the Son. This again establishes communication between them, refuting claims that they are the same. Consider the following verses:

At Jesus' Baptism

> *And lo a voice from heaven, saying, This is my beloved Son, in whom I am well pleased. Matt 3:17 (KJV)*

The Father speaks from heaven declaring Jesus as His Son that all may hear.

At His Transfiguration

> *While he yet spake, behold, a bright cloud overshadowed them: and*

> *behold a voice out of the cloud, which said, This is my beloved Son, in whom I am well pleased; hear ye him. Matt 17:5 (KJV)*

God speaks to the disciples at Jesus' transfiguration declaring that He is God's Son.

At Jesus' Entrance into Jerusalem

> *Now is my soul troubled; and what shall I say? Father, save me from this hour: but for this cause came I unto this hour. Father, glorify thy name. Then came there a voice from heaven, saying, I have both glorified it, and*

*will glorify it again. John 12:27-28 (KJV)*

Jesus prays to the Father and God responds to Him. Here is direct communication between the Father and the Son while Jesus lived as a man. Some try to purport that when Jesus, as a man, communicated and prayed to the Father, He was speaking to Himself.

If this were true, then God would have reduced Himself to parlor tricks and induce confusion in those that came to Him. Both Testaments are clear that the Father and the Son exist separately though they operate in total unity.

## The Progeny Spoke to the Progenitor

In addition to the record of the Father speaking to the Son, we have numerous New Testament accounts of Jesus, in his earthly ministry, speaking to the Father. However, the Old Testament gives us a few accounts of Christ speaking to the Father. David, in Psalm 40, gives us an account of Jesus speaking to the Father.

*Then said I, Lo, I come: in the volume of the book it is written of me, I delight to do thy will, O my God: yea, thy law is within my heart. Psalms 40:7-8 (KJV)*

Jesus speaks to the Father of the uselessness of sacrifice and burnt offerings and that He would come into the world to do the Father's will. The writer of Hebrews again helps us to understand that this truly is Christ speaking to God.

*Wherefore when he cometh into the world, he saith, Sacrifice and offering thou wouldest not, but a body hast thou prepared me: In burnt offerings and sacrifices for sin thou hast had no pleasure. Then said I, Lo, I come (in the volume of the book it is written of me,) to do thy will, O God. Heb 10:5-7 (KJV)*

The 'he' in this verse is Christ. He says these things unto God. Also, we discover here that Christ says that the Father prepared Him a body. We yet see Christ in subjection to the Father as an obedient Son.

We have stated that there are numerous accounts of the Son speaking to the Father while He walked the earth. But, there is one passage that must be considered in this section.

John 11 gives us the story of Lazarus' resurrection. Jesus' prayer at Lazarus' tomb help us to establish some truths previously discussed as well as demonstrate communication between the Father and the Son.

> *Then they took away the stone from the place where the dead was laid. And Jesus lifted up his eyes, and said, Father, I thank thee that thou hast heard me. And I knew that thou hearest me always: but because of the people which stand by I said it, that*

*they may believe that thou hast sent me. John 11:41-42 (KJV)*

In His prayer, Jesus establishes that He and the Father communicate. This is demonstrated by the words "thou hearest me always." This denotes continual communication.

In addition, at the end of His prayer, He states that He prayed to the Father that the people would believe that the Father sent Him. This again establishes that He and the Father are separate.

Though we have numerous references to communication between the Father and the Son, are there any scriptures that denote communication with the Holy Spirit? We learn from Jesus' words to the disciples that the Holy Spirit would never speak of Himself; whatever He hears that will He speak.

> *Howbeit when he, the Spirit of truth, is come, he will guide you into all truth: for he shall not speak of himself; but whatsoever he shall hear, that shall he speak: and he will shew you things to come. He shall glorify me: for he shall receive of mine, and shall shew*

*it unto you. John 16:13-14 (KJV)*

From this, we discover that the Holy Spirit is in constant communication with the Father. He can only speak once there has been communication from the Father and Son. Thus, we see continual communication in the heavens.

We can assuredly stand on the biblical truth that the Father, the Son, and the Holy Spirit each exist independently while operating as one. From this Lesson, we understand this truth for communication takes place between them.

This truth does not support the mythology of polytheism. It again establishes that the Father, the one true God, did all things as it has pleased Him through the Son and the Holy Spirit.

In our next Lesson, we will discuss Jesus as the Son of God. Though He is to be worshiped as God (by the Father's command), He abides continually as the Son.

If You Have Seen Me, You Have Seen the Father

**Notes:**

_____

_____

_____

_____

_____

_____

_____

_____

## If You Have Seen Me, You Have Seen the Father

If You Have Seen Me, You Have Seen the Father

# -Lesson 2-
# The Divine and the Disciples' Witness
## Psalm 2:7

If You Have Seen Me, You Have Seen the Father

Though Jesus Christ is worshiped as God, He eternally exists as the Son of God. This is a great mystery. How can God have a Son? As humans, we only understand parenthood in light of a birth.

Thus, the advocates of the Oneness doctrine use this limited concept to deny that Jesus is God's Son, eternally. They suppose that God calls Christ "Son" only because of the natural birth through Mary.

In this Lesson, we want to bring understanding to the Fatherhood of God and the Sonship of Christ. The scriptures are clear that Christ is the SON of God, not only when He came in the flesh, but eternally.

From the scriptures, we can assuredly state that Christ is the Son of God, thus, making Him separate from the Father. In the Law, every word (in terms of legal accusations and affirmations) was to be established by two or three witnesses.

*One witness shall not rise up against a man for any iniquity, or for any sin, in any sin that he sinneth: at the mouth of two witnesses, or at the mouth of three witnesses, shall the matter be established. Deut 19:15 (KJV)*

We have multiple biblical witnesses that Christ exists eternally as the Son of God. Again, this establishes His uniqueness in relation to the Father.

**The Witness of Fallen Angels**

Let us begin this section by understanding that we are never to formulate doctrine from the devil. However, from scriptural records, we see that the devil and demons know the truth concerning God and Christ.

The gospels attest that the Holy

Spirit led Jesus into the wilderness to be tempted of the devil. After fasting for forty days and nights, the devil appeared to test Him. In his attempts to defeat Christ, the devil opens his first two arguments by challenging the sonship of Christ.

*And when the tempter came to him, he said, If thou be the Son of God, command that these stones be made bread. Matt 4:3 (KJV)*

*And saith unto him, If thou be the Son of God, cast thyself down: for it is written, He shall give his angels charge concerning thee: and in their hands they shall bear thee up, lest at any time thou dash thy foot against a stone. Matt 4:6 (KJV)*

When the tempter appears, he calls Jesus' sonship into question. When individuals doubt that He is eternally the son of God, they are walking in the way of the enemy. If Jesus were not God's Son, the adversary would not have used that in his temptation of Christ.

But, the record shows that he did; affirming that God sent His Son, not that Jesus became His Son through birth. Not only did the devil recognize Christ as God's Son, but the demonic spirits that encountered Him also.

> *And when he was come to the other side into the country of the Gergesenes, there met him two possessed with devils, coming out of the tombs, exceeding fierce, so that no man might pass by that way. And, behold, they cried out, saying, What have we to do with thee, Jesus, thou Son of God? art thou come hither to torment us before the time? Matt 8:28-29 (KJV)*

*And unclean spirits, when they saw him, fell down before him, and cried, saying, Thou art the Son of God. Mark 3:11 (KJV)*

In each of the above passages, we discover that the demons called Jesus Christ the SON of God. In the case of the two demoniacs, they recognized Christ as God's Son in relation to eternal events.

They asked was the Son of God coming to torment them before the time. They recognized Christ as the Son of God who would judge all things in the end. This is why James wrote,

*Thou believest that there is one God; thou doest well: the devils also believe, and tremble.* James 2:19 (KJV)

James establishes the demonic forces' knowledge of the truth of God. He states that they believe that there is one God. We understand this to refer to the Father. Thus, when the demons encountered Christ, they called Him the Son of God rather than solely GOD.

## The Witness of God and Father

Some may argue that the above references do not substantiate the claim that Jesus is the Son of God. They may still want to assert that Christ was God the Father when He came in the flesh. However, the testimony of God is that Jesus Christ was and is His Son. They are not one and the same.

Again, considering Psalm 2, we discover that before Christ came in the flesh, God declared Him as Son.

*I will declare the decree: the LORD hath said unto me, Thou art my Son; this day have I begotten thee. Psalms 2:7 (KJV)*

Some of the Oneness advocates say

that this scripture is prophecy; that is, it is predicting Jesus Christ's birth through Mary as the Son of God. However, this is due to a misunderstanding of the word "begotten" and the expression "this day."

We stated at the beginning of this Lesson, that humans only understand parenthood and sonship in terms of natural childbirth. Hence, God declaring that He begat Christ seems only possible in light of Mary's delivery of Him. However, this is simply not the case.

The term "begotten" in the Hebrew carries different connotations. Therefore, in

Genesis, we find the generations of men recorded by listing fathers who begat children.

We know that men (males) do not have children, but their children are their offspring, lineage, heritage, and pedigree. This is the implication of "begotten" in Psalm 2. God was declaring Christ's pedigree and lineage, not His manner of birth.

In addition, begotten refers to Christ's being. He could only be the begotten of God through possessing the same attributes of God. Unlike the angels who were created, Christ was not a creation of God, but a reflection of Him.

> *Being made so much better than the angels, as he hath by inheritance obtained a more excellent name than they. For unto which of the angels said he at any time, Thou art my Son, this day have I begotten thee? And again, I will be to him a Father, and he shall be to me a Son? And again, when he bringeth in the firstbegotten into the world, he saith, And let all the angels of God worship him. Heb 1:4-6 (KJV)*

Christ was better than the angels because He was not created, but an eternal extension of God. The verse says God brought the first begotten into the world. Christ was the only begotten Son of God before His birth by Mary.

In understanding this, when God (in Psalm 2) says "this day," it is a prophetic denotation of time. As long as there is a day, God calls Christ His Son. Since God is eternal, the "day" never ends, so the sense of this verse reads, "You are My Son, eternally have I declared your lineage." God testifies that Christ is the Son for eternity.

In the book of Isaiah, it records that God's arm brought salvation to Israel.

> *And he saw that there was no man, and wondered that there was no intercessor: therefore, his arm brought salvation unto him; and his righteousness, it sustained him. Isaiah 59:16 (KJV)*

An arm is an extension of the body. It represents the body's strength and is made of the same substance of the body. The Oneness supporters say that this shows that God and Christ were one and that God was Israel's salvation personally.

Yet, this verse says His arm; that is an extension of Himself.

We know that this is a direct reflection of Christ. He came in the express image of God, reflecting God's strength, power, and personality. Since God is eternal, His arm is eternal; that is, Christ is eternal. He eternally exists as the Son: before His earthly appearance and after His resurrection.

Time would fail to list all the other scriptures of where the Father testifies of Christ as His Son. In Lesson 1, we discussed conversations between the Father and Son.

Listed there are other references to the Father's claim that Jesus was and is His Son. These only substantiate the Old Testament writings.

## The Witness of the Only Begotten

Some dishonest scholars and theologians have tried to assert that Jesus did not claim to be the Son of God. They say that Jesus only claimed to be the Son of Man.

A close examination of the gospels reveal otherwise. Jesus affirms that He is the Son of God. The gospel of John confirms this:

*Jesus heard that they had cast him out; and when he had found him, he said unto him, Dost thou believe on the Son of God? John 9:35 (KJV)*

*When Jesus heard that, he said, This sickness is not unto death, but for the glory of God, that the Son of God might be glorified thereby. John 11:4 (KJV)*

*Say ye of him, whom the Father hath sanctified, and sent into the world, Thou blasphemest; because I said, I am the Son of God? If I do not the works of my Father, believe me not. John 10:36-37 (KJV)*

Jesus not only referred to Himself as the Son of God, but also continually said that God was His Father in many passages. He clearly portrayed Himself as the Son of God. Even on the night that He was taken into custody Jesus said to the Father,

*And now, O Father, glorify thou me with thine own self with the glory which I had with thee before the world was. John 17:5 (KJV)*

These words of Christ's prayer

establish three truths. First, God is His Father. Second, Jesus possessed the same glory as the Father. Third, Jesus Christ was with God in eternity before all things. Thus, He established Himself eternally as the Son of God.

**The Witness of Christ's Messengers**

Jesus' followers also testified that Christ eternally exists as the Son of God. None of their writings promotes the Oneness doctrine; again that, He and the Father are the same. John wrote his gospel and his letters years after Christ's death and resurrection.

All his writings clearly affirmed that Christ (though He is to be served as Lord and God) is the Son of God. He wrote:

> *But these are written, that ye might believe that Jesus is the Christ, the Son of God; and that believing ye might have life through his name. John 20:31 (KJV)*
>
> *These things have I written unto you that believe on the name of the Son of God; that ye may know that ye have eternal life, and that ye may believe on the name of the Son of God. 1 John 5:13 (KJV)*

In his writings, John wrote to establish believers in the faith of the Son of God. There is no indication that Christ stop being God's Son after His work in the earth. The writings of all the other apostles also affirm Christ as the eternal Son of God.

In his opening statements in the Book of Romans, Paul establishes Christian thought, practice, and doctrine concerning God, Jesus, and their eternal relationship.

*Paul, a servant of Jesus Christ, called to be an apostle, separated unto the gospel of God, (Which he had promised afore by his prophets in the holy scriptures,) Concerning his Son Jesus Christ our Lord, which was made of the seed of David according to the flesh; And declared to be the Son of God with power, according to the spirit of holiness, by the resurrection from the dead. Romans 1:1-4 (KJV)*

In these lines, we discover that God has always preached the gospel through the prophets.

We learn that the gospel of God was concerning God's Son. The Holy Spirit's powerful ministry established and declared

Jesus to be the Son of God through the resurrection. Again, we see no evidence that Christ and God are one and the same, but that Jesus is God's only begotten Son. Peter's writings also support Christ as the eternal Son of God.

*Blessed be the God and Father of our Lord Jesus Christ... 1 Peter 1:3 (KJV)*

The tense of these words suggests that presently, God is the Father of Jesus. The writer of Hebrews also supports that Christ eternally exists as God's Son.

*God, who at sundry times and in divers manners spake in time past unto the fathers by the prophets, Hath in these last days spoken unto us by his Son...Heb 1:1-2 (KJV)*

Again, we see Christ as the Son of God. He was sent as the final revelation of the gospel of God. His life and ministry eternally speak to man for his redemption.

Therefore, we assuredly declare that Jesus eternally exists as the Son of God. When one believes on Christ, they believe on the name of the Son of God.

In our next Lesson, we will look closely at Jesus' sentiment, "If you have seen me, you have seen the Father." This has been the source of much debate and one of the chief scriptures used by the advocates of the Oneness doctrine.

However, we will prove that it does not suggest that Christ and God are the same, but that Christ truly came from God and is His Son.

If You Have Seen Me, You Have Seen the Father

If You Have Seen Me, You Have Seen the Father

**Notes**:

# If You Have Seen Me, You Have Seen the Father

If You Have Seen Me, You Have Seen the Father

# -Lesson 3-

# Views and Visions

John 14:9

If You Have Seen Me, You Have Seen the Father

Jesus' crucifixion was imminent. He told the disciples of His coming arrest and death. He warned Peter that he would deny Him. He reminds them of the hope of heaven.

Jesus reminded them that all who came to the Father had to come by Him. At this point, Philip asks Jesus to show the Father to them. It is here that we find these words,

> *Jesus saith unto him, Have I been so long time with you, and yet hast thou not known me, Philip? he that hath seen me hath seen the Father; and*

*how sayest thou then, Shew us the Father? John 14:9 (KJV)*

This response is one of the pillars of Oneness thought and doctrine, which seemingly poses a challenge to Trinitarianism. However, the gospels were not written to confuse, but to establish believers in the faith of the Son of God.

We established earlier that God, Christ, and the Holy Spirit were present in the beginning. God created all things by and through Christ. His command to make man in our image and after our likeness was not just rhetoric, but an acknowledgment of Christ who possessed the likeness and image of God.

We also discussed how there were conversations in heaven. Both Testaments reveal interaction between the Father and Son, establishing their individuality. Also, we learned that Christ is eternally the Son of God. Thus, Christ's words to Philip are recorded not to abolish the existence of the Father and Son concurrently, but to establish it.

How then should we regard His words? Without contradiction to the revelation of scriptures, Christ's words simply meant that anything they could learn and know of the Father had been demonstrated in His life. Hence, if you had seen Christ, you (really) had seen the Father.

Some might say, "No sir, you are putting a slant on His words!" However, if one continues to read the verses after this Jesus still refers to the Father as being distinct from Himself.

> *Believest thou not that I am in the Father, and the Father in me? the words that I speak unto you I speak not of myself: but the Father that*

*dwelleth in me, he doeth the works. Believe me that I am in the Father, and the Father in me: or else believe me for the very works' sake. John 14:10-11 (KJV)*

Jesus says that all that He preached and performed was because of the Father. When He states that the Father is in Him and He is in the Father, He was not making a theological statement concerning literal oneness, but of how He and the Father are in total agreement.

As Christians, we are said to be the Body of Christ and to be one with Him.

However, we retain our individuality though we abide in Him. This is the same principle with Jesus and the Father. Yet, some will still say that this is a matter of interpretation. Well, let us look to the scriptures to establish the presented viewpoint.

## Daniel's Coronation Vision

We discovered that the Hebraic use of the term elohim to describe God was not in reference to His plurality, but to His supremacy above anything that is called 'god.' The Hebrews were to worship only one God.

We know in hindsight from the New Testament that the one true God sent His Son who is to be worshiped in honor of God. Though the full revelation of Christ was to come, God still spoke to the prophets of Christ's coming and rule.

The Book of Daniel contains profound visions and prophecies of the end times. Daniel's visions told of Christ's earthly ministry as well as His eternal rule with the Father.

It is from this, we discover one of the greatest truths, which gives clear evidence of the intent of Christ's statement, "he that hath seen me, hath seen the Father."

> *I beheld till the thrones were cast down, and the Ancient of days did sit, whose garment was white as snow, and the hair of his head like the pure wool: his throne was like the fiery flame, and his wheels as burning fire.* Dan 7:9 (KJV)

Daniel's vision foretells the culmination of all things and places God the Father, sitting on the throne. We see two descriptors of His appearance: garment white as snow and hair was like pure wool. Continuing, Daniel reveals that the Ancient of days is giving power, dominion, and authority to another.

> *I saw in the night visions, and, behold, one like the Son of man came with the clouds of heaven, and came to the Ancient of days, and they brought him near before him. And there was given him dominion, and glory, and a kingdom, that all people, nations, and languages, should serve him: his dominion is an everlasting dominion, which shall not pass away, and his*

*kingdom that which shall not be destroyed. Dan 7:13-14 (KJV)*

Without contradiction, we understand that this is a clear reference to Jesus Christ. He called Himself the "Son of man" repeatedly. Hence, we discover that Christ is to be worshipped because God gave dominion to Him. Also, we see God and Christ existing distinctly; that is, separately in heaven.

The appearance of Christ on earth was not a modalistic act of God, He was the Son of God coming in the name of His Father. Because of His obedience and submission, all are to worship, honor, and adore Him in obedience and to the glory of the one true God.

*And that every tongue should confess that Jesus Christ is Lord, to the glory of God the Father. Phil 2:11 (KJV)*

This is the mystery of how Christians are monotheistic. The one true God commands men to honor and worship His Son. When we worship Christ, it brings honor and glory to God.

Before proceeding further, we want to focus on the two descriptors given of

God's appearance. Again, He is said to be clothed in a white garment, with hair as white as wool. Now, let us look at John's description of Christ given in Revelation, chapter 1.

> *And in the midst of the seven candlesticks one like unto the Son of man, clothed with a garment down to the foot, and girt about the paps with a golden girdle. His head and his hairs were white like wool, as white as snow; and his eyes were as a flame of fire. Rev 1:13-14 (KJV)*

When comparing these two passages, we discover that Jesus Christ and the Father share identical characteristics with some distinctions placed upon Christ. Each possessed hair as wool and a long white garment. This helps us to grasp further Jesus' statements to Philip.

Even in Christ's appearance to John, He was revealing what the Father was like. This demonstrates again the oneness of God and Christ. Jesus' statement does not establish that He and the Father are one and the same, but it does establish that

Christ was with God, came from God, and that He is God's Son.

Thus, to behold Him is to behold the Father because He came from Him.

## Jesus' View of His Commission

The flaw of some biblical interpretation is that it is tainted by an individual's perspective rather than by the biblical narrative. We stated earlier that Christ's words did not come to confuse but establish truth.

To understand His words, we must consider Christ's perspective and not our personal opinions. Throughout His ministry, Jesus declared that everything that He did was in submission and obedience to the Father. He said that His word and doctrine were from the Father.

*For I have not spoken of myself; but the Father which sent me, he gave me a commandment, what I should say, and what I should speak. John 12:49 (KJV)*

Jesus attributed the healings, miracles, and many wonderful works to the Father.

*But Jesus answered them, My Father worketh hitherto, and I work. Then answered Jesus and said unto them, Verily, verily, I say unto you, The Son can do nothing of himself, but what he seeth the Father do: for what things soever he doeth, these also doeth the Son likewise. John 5:17, 19 (KJV)*

Christ makes many similar statements during His ministry. These form the foundation for His statement to Philip. Christ testified that He said and did all things at the Father's command. Whatever He saw the Father doing that is what He did. His life was a demonstration of the Father at work.

Consequently, for Philip to ask Him to show the Father to them was an ill-advised request. They had seen the Father working through Christ the entire time and had not realized it. Therefore, His statement only verifies this truth, not that He and the Father are one and the same.

**The Apostles' View of the Divine Persons**

The apostles' teachings on the relationship between Christ and God establish our argument thus far. They taught that (as Jesus said) to behold Christ was to see the Father; that is, His nature,

His divinity, and His will. Paul wrote these words,

> *In whom we have redemption through his blood, even the forgiveness of sins: Who is the image of the invisible God, the firstborn of every creature: Col 1:14-15 (KJV)*

Christ came in the image of the invisible God. What could be learned of God was revealed in Christ. The writer of Hebrews asserts the same argument.

> *Who being the brightness of his glory, and the express image of his person, and upholding all things by*

*the word of his power, when he had by himself purged our sins, sat down on the right hand of the Majesty on high. Heb 1:3 (KJV)*

Not only is Christ seen as the express image of God, but He also is seen seated at God's right hand. If they were one and the same, this statement would be ridiculous. John establishes our present affirmations also.

*No man hath seen God at any time; the only begotten Son, which is in the bosom of the Father, he hath declared him. John 1:18 (KJV)*

No man has even seen God. In the Old Testament, men would only have visions of the Father where His face and His form could not be fully described because of His brightness. Consider Ezekiel's description.

> *and upon the likeness of the throne was the likeness as the appearance of a man above upon it... from the appearance of his loins even upward, and from the appearance of his loins even downward... Ezek 1:26-27 (KJV)*

In addition, God's words and prophetic counsel were filtered through the prophets and the teachings of the Law, which could add to ambiguity, obscurity, and uncertainty.

Thus, Christ came to show the Father to the world, in all His glory, to those who would receive Him. To receive Christ, was and is to receive the Father. This is the underlying context of Christ's statements to Philip.

There was no need of another vision or interpretation of the Law because Christ was not only the Son of God, but also as the Word made flesh. His life and ministry were the perfect reflection of the fullness of God. Jesus conveyed to Philip that God placed all things upon Him and that they did not need to look for anything else.

*We are in Union (Matthew 10:30).* This profound statement of Christ is a key thread in the Oneness doctrine and could be a potential flaw in the Trinitarian doctrine. However, this statement was not made to support or refute either doctrine, but to establish the relationship between the Father and the Son. We will look at this from a natural standpoint to verify the truth and meaning of Jesus' words.

> *I desired Titus, and with him I sent a brother. Did Titus make a gain of you? walked we not in the same spirit? walked we not in the same steps? 2 Cor 12:18 (KJV)*

In his letter to the Corinthians, Paul states that he sent one of his sons in the ministry, Titus. Then, that Titus walked in the same spirit and steps as Paul. Paul was saying that Titus did not say or do anything differently from what he would do.

Now, if one could speak of another human, who is subject to error in this manner, how much the more could this be said of Christ in relation to God? Christ walked as the Father would walk and came in the same Spirit of the Father. There is no division in what God wants and what the Son wants. Therefore, Christ and the Father are one: in spiritual essence and form, and in personality, volition, intent, and will.

Besides, in the verses before and after, Jesus continues to make a distinction between Himself and the Father. Hence, this statement does not speak to the numerical value of Him and the Father, but their union (as the Greek word for "one" in this verse (Mtt. 10:30 illustrates).

Therefore, we understand through biblical insight that if one beheld Christ, He did behold the Father, though they are distinct. Without contradiction and controversy, the Father and Son exist independently, yet succinctly.

If You Have Seen Me, You Have Seen the Father

**Notes**:

## If You Have Seen Me, You Have Seen the Father

## If You Have Seen Me, You Have Seen the Father

# Bibliography

**Merriam-Webster Online Dictionary.** Copyright © 2005 by Merriam-Webster, Incorporated. All rights reserved.

**The Bible Library.** Copyright 1988 – 2000. Ellis Enterprises Incorporated, 4205 McAuley Blvd., Suite 385, Oklahoma City, OK 73120, (405) 749-0273. All Rights Reserved.

**Lockman Foundation.** *Comparative Study Bible.* Zondervan Publishing House. Grand Rapids, MI, c1984

**Smith, William.** *Smith's Bible Dictionary.* Holman Bible Publishers. Nashville, TN. c1994

## Notes:

## If You Have Seen Me, You Have Seen the Father